CELEBRATING ALL FRIENDS

THE PEANUT PROBLEM

OUR FRIEND KENJI HAS A FOOD ALLERGY

by Kirsten McDonald
illustrated by Michael Emmerson

GRASSHOPPER

Tools for Parents & Teachers

Grasshopper Books enhance imagination and introduce the earliest readers to fiction with fun storylines and illustrations. The easy-to-read text supports early reading experiences with repetitive sentence patterns and sight words.

Before Reading

- Discuss the cover illustration. What do readers see?
- Look at the picture glossary together. Discuss the words.

Read the Book

- Read the book to the child, or have him or her read independently.
- "Walk" through the book and look at the illustrations. Who is the main character? What is happening in the story?

After Reading

- Prompt the child to think more. Ask: Kenji has a food allergy. Do you know anyone with a food allergy? What do they do to stay safe?

Grasshopper Books are published by Jump!
5357 Penn Avenue South
Minneapolis, MN 55419
www.jumplibrary.com

Library of Congress Cataloging-in-Publication Data

Names: McDonald, Kirsten, author.
Emmerson, Michael, illustrator.
Title: The peanut problem : our friend Kenji has a food allergy / by Kirsten McDonald; Michael Emmerson.
Description: Minneapolis, MN: Jump!, Inc., [2024]
Series: Celebrating all friends | Includes index.
Audience: Ages 7-10
Identifiers: LCCN 2023000528 (print)
LCCN 2023000529 (ebook)
ISBN 9798885248891 (hardcover)
ISBN 9798885248907 (paperback)
ISBN 9798885248914 (ebook)
Subjects: CYAC: Food allergy–Fiction. | Peanuts–Fiction.
Friendship–Fiction. | LCGFT: Picture books.
Classification: LCC PZ7.1.M4344 Pea 2024 (print)
LCC PZ7.1.M4344 (ebook)
DDC [E] –dc23
LC record available at https://lccn.loc.gov/2023000528
LC ebook record available at https://lccn.loc.gov/2023000529

Editor: Eliza Leahy
Direction and Layout: Anna Peterson
Illustrator: Michael Emmerson

Printed in the United States of America at Corporate Graphics in North Mankato, Minnesota.

Table of Contents

Keeping Kenji Safe

“What do you have today?”
Emily asks at lunchtime.

"Noodles," says Kenji. "They're my favorite."

"I have my favorite," says Amir.

Emily says, "I have my favorite, too—a peanut butter sandwich."

"Oh, no!" says Kenji. "I have a peanut allergy. Even a tiny bit of peanut butter can make my throat swell so I can't breathe. If that happens, I have to use my EpiPen."

"What is an EpiPen?" asks Amir.

"It's a shot like you get at the doctor's," says Kenji. "One time at a restaurant, I accidentally ate some peanuts. My mom used my EpiPen on me so I could breathe."

"I don't want you to need your EpiPen!" says Emily. "I will sit with Katie today."

"Thanks for being safe," Kenji says. "Let's sit together tomorrow."

"I like your necklace," Amir says.

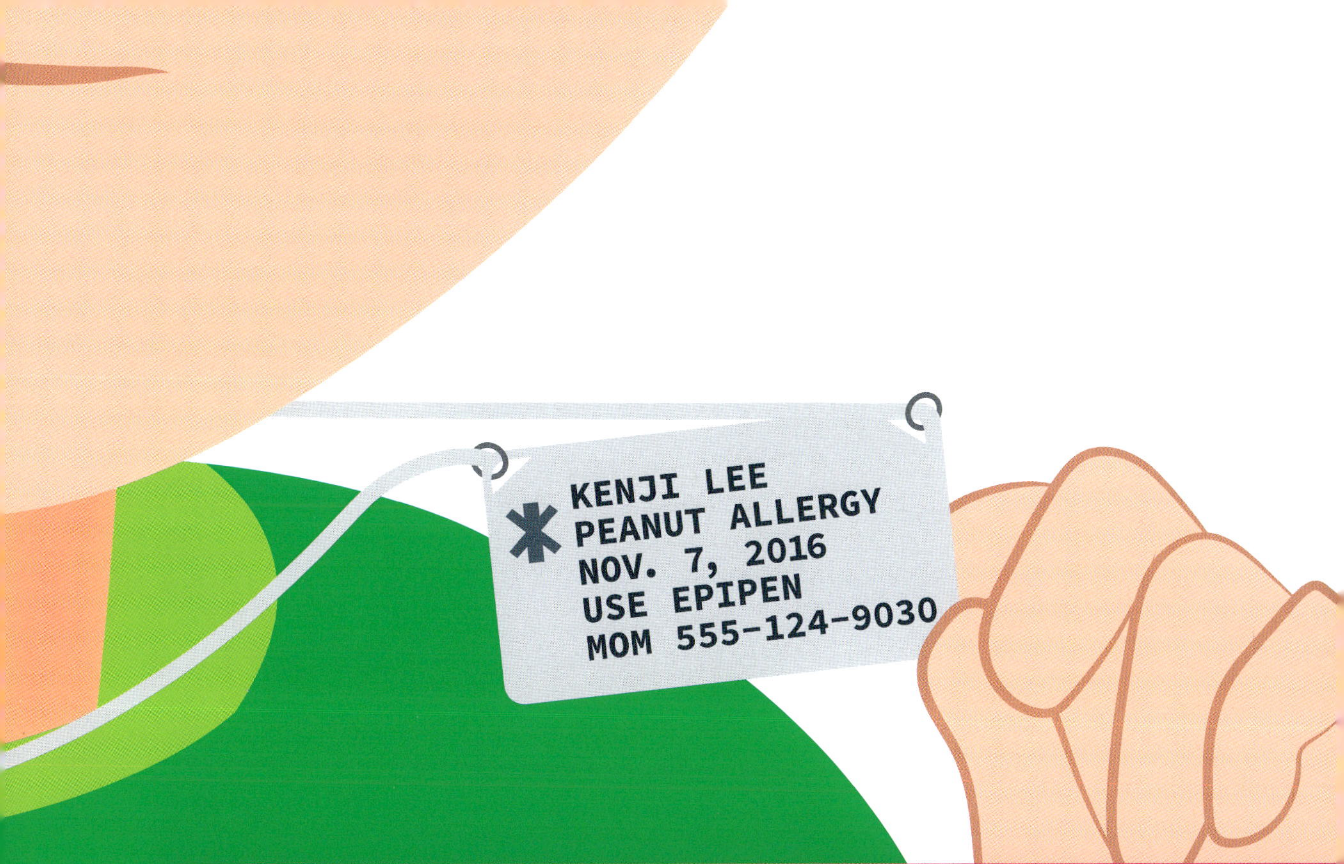

"Thanks!" says Kenji. "It's my med-alert necklace. It says I have a peanut allergy. It lists my name, birthday, and my mom's phone number. I wear it in case my allergy causes an emergency."

After lunch, Emily says, "Everyone, please wash your hands. Some people have food allergies. The tiniest bit of peanut butter can make them sick."

"Thanks for reminding us," says Mrs. Clement.

"I'm glad you told me about your food allergy," Emily says later that day.

"Thanks for understanding," says Kenji.

At art time, Amir says, “Let’s make posters to remind everyone not to bring peanuts to school.”

“That’s a great idea,” says Mrs. Clement.

The students hang the posters around the school.

The next day at lunch, Kenji, Amir, and Emily sit together.

"No peanuts today!" Emily says.

"Me either," says Amir.

"And none for me ever!" says Kenji.

Let's Review!

Amir and Emily help their friend Kenji with his peanut allergy. How do they help him? What are some things you can do to help people with food allergies?

tell others

wash your hands

bring safe food to eat

Quiz Time!

What tools help Kenji in an emergency? Point to all that are true.

a. EpiPen

b. peanuts

c. med-alert necklace

d. posters

Quiz Time! Answer Key: **a** and **c**

Picture Glossary

allergy
A medical condition in which one's body thinks something is harmful and reacts by causing them to be sick, get itchy, or stop breathing.

emergency
A sudden and dangerous situation that requires fast action.

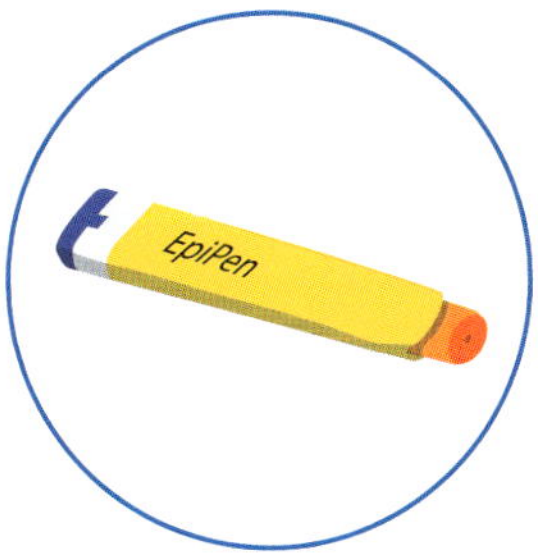

EpiPen
An easy-to-use shot that can stop a bad allergic reaction.

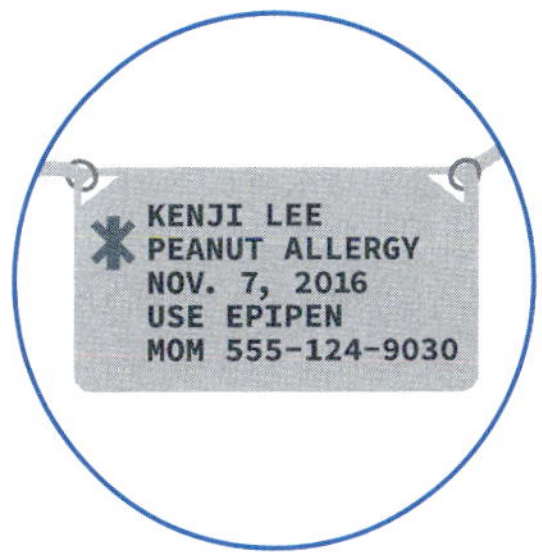

med-alert necklace
A special necklace with information about a serious medical condition.

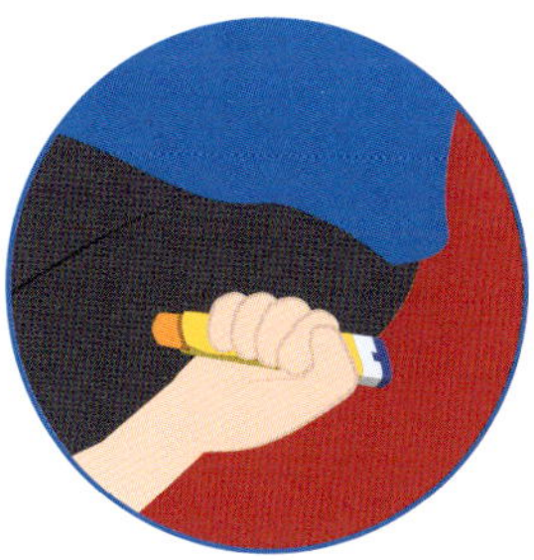

shot
An injection of medicine into the body.

swell
To puff out and take up more space.

Index

To Learn More

FACT SURFER

Finding more information is as easy as 1, 2, 3.

1. Go to www.factsurfer.com
2. Enter "**thepeanutproblem**" into the search box.
3. Choose your book to see a list of websites.